KNOCK-KNOCK JOKES FOR FUNNY KIDS

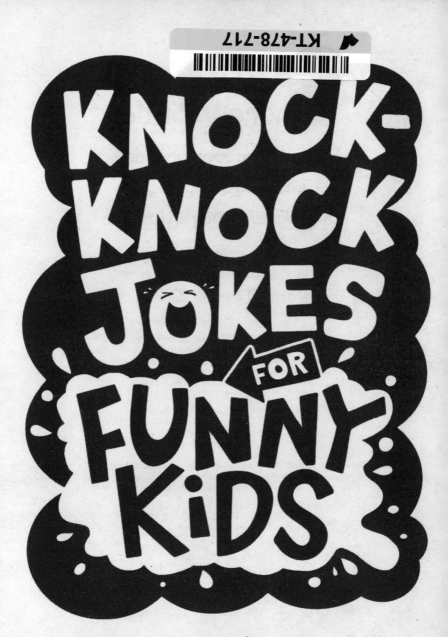

Buster Books

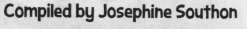

Illustrated by
Andrew Pinder

Compiled by Josephine Southon

Edited by Jonny Leighton

Designed by Derrian Bradder

First published in Great Britain in 2021 by Buster Books,
an imprint of Michael O'Mara Books Limited,
9 Lion Yard, Tremadoc Road, London SW4 7NQ

W www.mombooks.com/buster   f Buster Books   🐦 @BusterBooks   📷 @buster_books

A CIP catalogue record for this book is available from the British Library.

ISBN: 978-1-78055-785-4

2 4 6 8 10 9 7 5 3 1

Papers used by Buster Books are natural, recyclable products made of wood from
well-managed, FSC®-certified forests and other controlled sources. The manufacturing
processes conform to the environmental regulations of the country of origin.

Printed and bound in September 2021 by CPI Group (UK) Ltd,
108 Beddington Lane, Croydon, CR0 4YY, United Kingdom

FSC
www.fsc.org
MIX
Paper from
responsible sources
FSC® C020471

CONTENTS

Introduction

Knock Knock!

Who's there?

Juno.

Juno, who?

Juno how funny this book is?

Welcome to this te-he-he-larious collection of the best knock-knock jokes for funny kids.

In this book you will find over 200 hilarious knock-knock jokes, featuring spooky ghosts and ghouls, wild and wily animals, silly sporting moments and much much more.

If these jokes don't tickle your funny bone then nothing will. Don't forget to share the best ones with your friends and family so you can practise your comic timing.

Ghoulish Giggles

Knock Knock!

Who's there?

Fangs.

Fangs, who?

Fangs for letting me in.

Knock Knock!

Who's there?

Ivan.

Ivan, who?

Ivan to suck your blood!

Knock Knock!

Who's there?

Wanda.

Wanda, who?

Wanda watch a scary movie tonight?

Knock Knock!

Who's there?

Vampire.

Vampire, who?

The Vampire State Building, of course!

Knock Knock!

Who's there?

Frank.

Frank, who?

Frankenstein's monster, RARRR!

Knock Knock!

Who's there?

Witches.

Witches, who?

Witches the way to the graveyard?

Knock Knock!

Who's there?

Boo.

Boo, who?

Don't cry, I'm not a real ghost!

Knock Knock!

Who's there?

The ghost.

The ghost, who?

The ghost is clear, you can come in.

Knock Knock!

Who's there?

Ice Cream.

Ice cream, who?

Ice cream every
time I see a ghost.

Knock Knock!

Who's there?

Tyson.

Tyson, who?

Tyson garlic around
your neck to keep
vampires away.

Knock Knock!

Who's there?

Bee.

Bee, who?

Bee-ware, it's a full moon tonight.

Knock Knock!

Who's there?

Werewolf.

Werewolf, who?

Where wolf I find the bathroom please?

Knock Knock!

Who's there?

Rick.

Rick, who?

Rick or treat!

Knock Knock!

Who's there?

Phillip.

Phillip, who?

Phillip my bag with Halloween treats, please.

Knock Knock!

Who's there?

Werewolves.

Werewolves, who?

**Werewolves who say,
"Happy Howl-oween!"**

Knock Knock!

Who's there?

Esme.

Esme, who?

**Esme bag full of
chocolate yet?**

Knock Knock!

Who's there?

Juan.

Juan, who?

The Juan-eyed monster.

Knock Knock!

Who's there?

Witch.

Witch, who?

Witch one of you can fix my broomstick?

Knock Knock!

Who's there?

Chuck.

Chuck, who?

Just Chuck-ing to see if there are any zombies outside.

Knock Knock!

Who's there?

Orange.

Orange, who?

Orange ya glad I didn't say zombie?

15

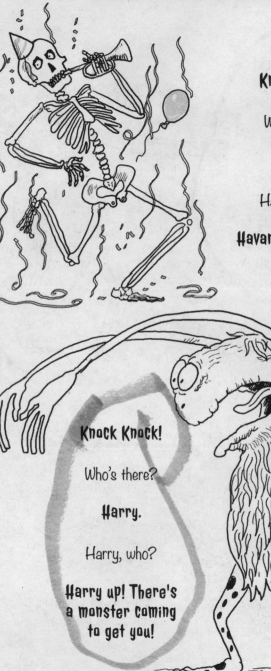

Knock Knock!

Who's there?

Havana.

Havana, who?

Havana spooky time.

Knock Knock!

Who's there?

Harry.

Harry, who?

Harry up! There's a monster coming to get you!

Knock Knock!

Who's there?

Diane.

Diane, who?

I'm Diane to meet you.

Knock Knock!

Who's there?

Bee.

Bee, who?

Bee-ware of witches on Halloween!

Animal Antics

Knock Knock!

Who's there?

Cows go.

Cows go, who?

No, cows go moo, silly.

Knock Knock!

Who's there?

Pasture.

Pasture, who?

Pasture bedtime, isn't it?

Knock Knock!

Who's there?

Chick.

Chick, who?

Chick your oven, something's burning!

Knock Knock!

Who's there?

Interrupting sloth.

Interrupting sloth, who?

...

No, really, interrupting sloth, wh—

Slooooth.

20

Knock Knock!

Who's there?

Alpaca.

Alpaca, who?

Alpaca the suitcase, you load the car.

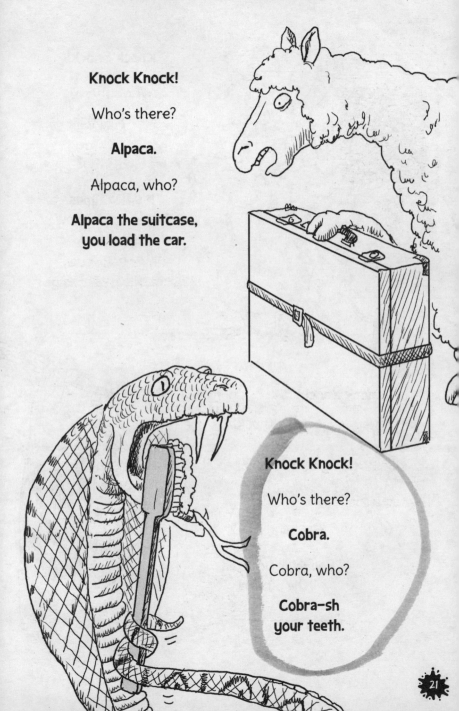

Knock Knock!

Who's there?

Cobra.

Cobra, who?

Cobra–sh your teeth.

Knock Knock!

Who's there?

Flea.

Flea, who?

**It's flea times
I've knocked, now.
Let me in!**

Knock Knock!

Who's there?

Beehive.

Beehive, who?

**Bee-hive yourself
little buzzer!**

Knock Knock!

Who's there?

Owls say.

Owls say, who?

Yes, they do.

Knock Knock!

Who's there?

Oink oink.

Oink oink, who?

Make up your mind, are you a pig or an owl?

Knock Knock!

Who's there?

Some bunny.

Some bunny, who?

Some–bunny has been eating my carrots.

Knock Knock!

Who's there?

Viper.

Viper, who?

Viper nose, it's running.

Knock Knock!

Who's there?

Yvette.

Yvette, who?

Yvette is great with animals.

Knock Knock!

Who's there?

Abbie.

Abbie, who?

Abbie stung me on the arm.

25

Knock Knock!

Who's there?

Rhino.

Rhino, who?

Rhino how to make you laugh!

Knock Knock!

Who's there?

Thea.

Thea, who?

Thea later, alligator.

Knock Knock!

Who's there?

Herd.

Herd, who?

Herd you were home, want to hang out?

Knock Knock!

Who's there?

Lion.

Lion, who?

Lion on your doorstep, open up!

Knock Knock!

Who's there?

Moose.

Moose, who?

**Moose you
be so nosy?**

Knock Knock!

Who's there?

Patsy.

Patsy, who?

**Patsy dog on the
head, he likes it.**

Knock Knock!

Who's there?

Iguana.

Iguana, who?

Iguana hold your hand.

Knock Knock!

Who's there?

Goat.

Goat, who?

Goat to the door and find out.

29

Knock Knock!

Who's there?

Quiche.

Quiche, who?

Can I have a hug
and quiche?

Knock Knock!

Who's there?

Banana.

Banana, who?

Knock Knock!

Who's there?

Orange.

Orange, who?

Orange you glad I
didn't say banana!

Knock Knock!

Who's there?

Lettuce.

Lettuce, who?

Lettuce in, it's cold out here.

Knock Knock!

Who's there?

Bean.

Bean, who?

Bean a while since I last saw you.

Knock Knock!

Who's there?

Pasta.

Pasta, who?

Pasta salt, please.

Knock Knock!

Who's there?

Turnip.

Turnip, who?

Turnip the heat, it's cold in here.

Knock Knock!

Who's there?

Peas.

Peas, who?

Peas to meet you.

Knock Knock!

Who's there?

Butter.

Butter, who?

Butter bring an umbrella, it looks like it might rain.

Knock Knock!

Who's there?

Anita.

Anita, who?

Anita another napkin.

Knock Knock!

Who's there?

Arthur.

Arthur, who?

Arthur any more cookies?

Knock Knock!

Who's there?

Albie.

Albie, who?

**Albie in the kitchen
if you need me.**

Knock Knock!

Who's there?

Philippa.

Philippa, who?

**Philippa glass
and join me!**

Knock Knock!

Who's there?

Geno.

Geno, who?

Geno, I don't like broccoli.

Knock Knock!

Who's there?

Abbott.

Abbott, who?

Abbott time to eat isn't it?

Knock Knock!

Who's there?

Aida.

Aida, who?

**Aida lot of chocolate
and now I feel sick.**

Knock Knock!

Who's there?

Hammond.

Hammond, who?

**Hammond eggs for
breakfast please!**

Knock Knock!

Who's there?

Handsome.

Handsome, who?

**Hand-some pizza
to me, please.**

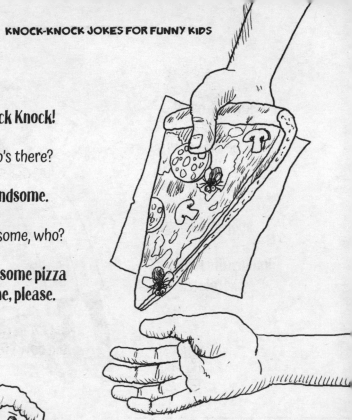

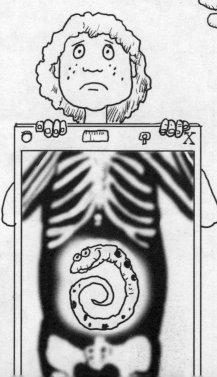

Knock Knock!

Who's there?

Henrietta.

Henrietta, who?

**Henrietta worm that
was in her apple.**

Knock Knock!

Who's there?

Imogen.

Imogen, who?

Imogen life without chocolate!

Knock Knock!

Who's there?

Lenny.

Lenny, who?

Lenny in, I'm hungry!

40

Knock Knock!

Who's there?

Noah.

Noah, who?

Noah good restaurant around here?

Knock Knock!

Who's there?

Sid.

Sid, who?

Sid down and have a cup of coffee.

Space Sillies

Knock Knock!

Who's there?

Alien.

Alien, who?

Just how many aliens do you know?

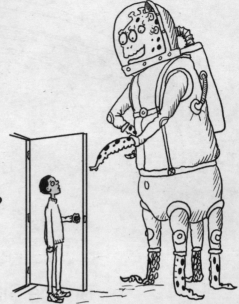

Knock Knock!

Who's there?

Armageddon.

Armageddon, who?

Armageddon a little bored, want to play a game?

Knock Knock!

Who's there?

Sunny.

Sunny, who?

Sunny you should ask.

Knock Knock!

Who's there?

Saturn.

Saturn, who?

Sa—turn that frown upside down!

Knock Knock!

Who's there?

Apollo.

Apollo, who?

Apollo–gies for disturbing you.

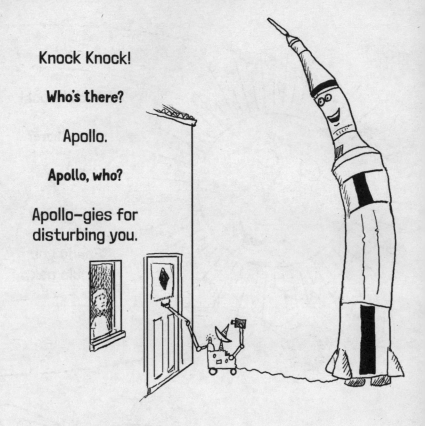

Knock Knock!

Who's there?

Lunar.

Lunar, who?

Lunar or later you'll have to let me in.

Knock Knock!

Who's there?

Titan.

Titan, who?

Titan your seatbelt, it's going to be a bumpy ride.

Knock Knock!

Who's there?

Crater.

Crater, who?

Crater meet you.

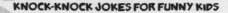

Knock Knock!

Who's there?

Meteor.

Meteor, who?

Meteor your
new neighbour!

Knock Knock!

Who's there?

Comet.

Comet, who?

Comet book.
Wanna read?

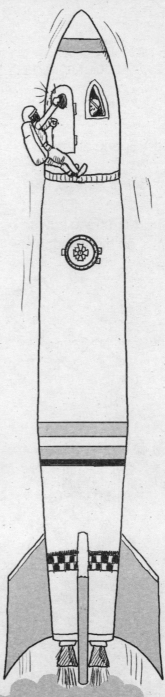

Knock Knock!

Who's there?

Les.

Les, who?

Les go to the space centre today.

Knock Knock!

Who's there?

Launch.

Launch, who?

Launch break soon, I'm starving!

Knock Knock!

Who's there?

Space cows go.

Space cows go, who?

No, space cows
go moooooon.

Knock Knock!

Who's there?

Hubble.

Hubble, who?

Hubble, hubble,
toil and trouble.

Knock Knock!

Who's there?

UV.

UV, who?

What UV is
what you get.

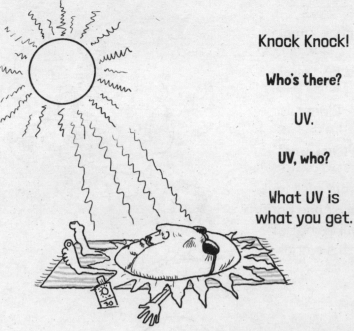

Knock Knock!

Who's there?

Rays.

Rays, who?

Rays and shine,
sleepyhead!

Knock Knock!

Who's there?

Planet.

Planet, who?

Planet well and your space party will be out of this world!

Knock Knock!

Who's there?

Neptune.

Neptune, who?

I Nep-tuned out for a second there, what did you say?

52

Knock Knock!

Who's there?

Rocket.

Rocket, who?

Rocket gently and
the baby will
fall asleep.

Knock Knock!

Who's there?

Solar.

Solar, who?

Sol-are we
going to the
park or what?

Knock Knock!

Who's there?

Orbit.

Orbit, who?

I'm or–bit hungry, do you have any food?

Knock Knock!

Who's there?

Venus.

Venus, who?

Venus get a doorbell.

Knock Knock!

Who's there?

Five, four, three.

Five, four, three, who?

Five, four, three, who, one. Lift off!

Knock Knock!

Who's there?

Shuttle.

Shuttle, who?

I'll shuttle up with the knock-knock jokes now.

Knock Knock!

Who's there?

Jo.

Jo, who?

Jo King.

Knock Knock!

Who's there?

Sven.

Sven, who?

Sven are you going to open the door?

Knock Knock!

Who's there?

Anita.

Anita, who?

Anita drink of
water, let me in!

Knock Knock!

Who's there?

Candice.

Candice, who?

Candice joke get
any worse?

Knock Knock!

Who's there?

Al.

Al, who?

Al give you a
high five if you
open the door.

Knock Knock!

Who's there?

Alex.

Alex, who?

Alex the questions
around here.

Knock Knock!

Who's there?

Annie.

Annie, who?

Annie body going to open the door?

Knock Knock!

Who's there?

Claire.

Claire, who?

Claire the way, I'm coming in.

Knock Knock!

Who's there?

Doris.

Doris, who?

Doris locked,
open up please.

Knock Knock!

Who's there?

Ash.

Ash, who?

Bless you!

Knock Knock!

Who's there?

Champ.

Champ, who?

Champ-poo your hair,
it's getting dirty!

Knock Knock!

Who's there?

Doug.

Doug, who?

A Doug is a man's
best friend!

Knock Knock!

Who's there?

Luke.

Luke, who?

Luke through the keyhole and you'll see.

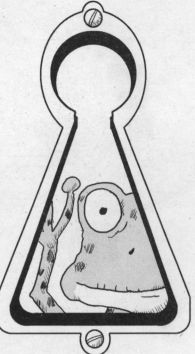

Knock Knock!

Who's there?

Mikey.

Mikey, who?

Mikey doesn't fit in the door.

Knock Knock!

Who's there?

Amanda.

Amanda, who?

**Amanda fix
the plumbing!**

Knock Knock!

Who's there?

Isma.

Isma, who?

**Isma dinner
ready yet?**

Knock Knock!

Who's there?

Ed.

Ed, who?

Ed rather not say.

Knock Knock!

Who's there?

In a while.

In a while, who?

In a while, crocodile.

Knock Knock!

Who's there?

Stan.

Stan, who?

Stan back, I'm coming through!

Knock Knock!

Who's there?

Avery.

Avery, who?

A-very nice person knocking on your door.

Knock Knock!

Who's there?

Rupert.

Rupert, who?

Rupert your left foot in, your left foot out, in, out, in, out and shake it all about ...

Knock Knock!

Who's there?

Rhoda.

Rhoda, who?

Row, row, Rhoda boat, gently down the stream ...

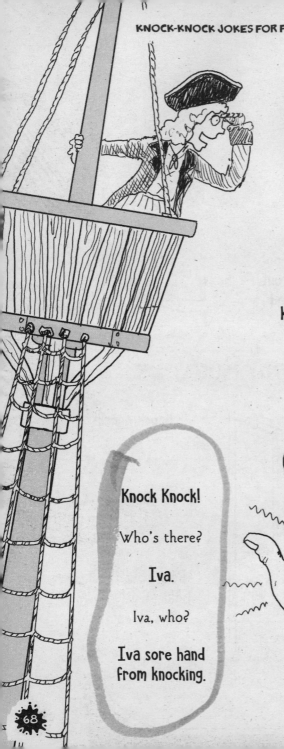

Knock Knock!

Who's there?

Luke.

Luke, who?

Luke out, here comes another knock-knock joke!

Knock Knock!

Who's there?

Iva.

Iva, who?

Iva sore hand from knocking.

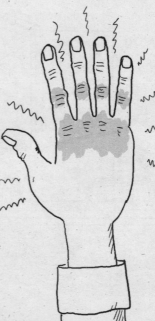

Random Roarers

Knock Knock!

Who's there?

Quiet Tina.

Quiet Tina, who?

Quiet Tina library, shhh.

Knock Knock!

Who's there?

Olive.

Olive, who?

Olive nextdoor. Nice to meet you!

Knock Knock!

Who's there?

Europe.

Europe, who?

No, you're a poo!

Knock Knock!

Who's there?

Choo.

Choo, who?

Choo-choo train!

Knock Knock!

Who's there?

Venice.

Venice, who?

Venice the pizza delivery arriving?

Knock Knock!

Who's there?

Accordion.

Accordion, who?

Accordion to the weather channel, it's going to be sunny tomorrow.

Knock Knock!

Who's there?

Turnip.

Turnip, who?

**Turnip the music,
I love this song.**

Knock Knock!

Who's there?

Will.

Will, who?

**Will you let me
in already?**

Knock Knock!

Who's there?

Fiddle.

Fiddle, who?

If fiddle make you happy, I'll tell you.

Knock Knock!

Who's there?

Chopin.

Chopin, who?

Chopin at the market, want to come?

Knock Knock!

Who's there?

Sudden dramatic music.

Sudden dramatic music wh—

DUN, DUN DUUUUNNN.

Knock Knock!

Who's there?

Nadia.

Nadia, who?

Nadia head when the music plays!

Knock Knock!

Who's there?

Thor.

Thor, who?

I've got a Thor tongue. I bit it by mistake.

Knock Knock!

Who's there?

Sir.

Sir, who?

Sir Cumference.

Knock Knock!

Who's there?

Tennis.

Tennis, who?

Tennis five plus five.

Knock Knock!

Who's there?

Kanga.

Kanga, who?

No, it's kangaroo!

Knock Knock!

Who's there?

A little old lady.

A little old lady, who?

I didn't know you could yodel.

Knock Knock!

Who's there?

Cargo.

Cargo, who?

No, car go BEEP BEEP!

Knock Knock!

Who's there?

Leaf.

Leaf, who?

Leaf me alone!

Knock Knock!

Who's there?

Dishes.

Dishes, who?

**Dishes the police,
open up!**

Knock Knock!

Who's there?

Cash.

Cash, who?

No thanks, I prefer hazelnuts.

Knock Knock!

Who's there?

Interrupting cow.

Interrupting cow, wh—?

Moooooooo.

Historical
Howlers

Knock Knock!

Who's there?

King Tut.

King Tut, who?

King Tut-key
fried chicken.

Knock Knock!

Who's there?

Sphinx.

Sphinx, who?

She Sphinx she's the
best, that Cleopatra.

Knock Knock!

Who's there?

A Mayan.

A Mayan, who?

A Mayan the way standing here?

Knock Knock!

Who's there?

Anne Boleyn.

Anne Boleyn, who?

There's Anne Boleyn alley down the road, want to go?

84

Knock Knock!

Who's there?

Queen.

Queen, who?

Queen yourself. I can smell you through the door!

Knock Knock!

Who's there?

Albert Einstein.

Albert Einstein, who?

Albert Einstein's brother, Frank Einstein ... Grr!

Knock Knock!

Who's there?

Abraham Lincoln

Abraham Lincoln, who?

Pfft. You really don't know who I am?

Knock Knock!

Who's there?

Tudors.

Tudors, who?

There's tudors on your house, which one should I use?

Knock Knock!

Who's there?

Warrior.

Warrior, who?

Warrior been
all my life?

Knock Knock!

Who's there?

Knight.

Knight, who?

Knight knight,
time for bed.

Knock Knock!

Who's there?

Odysseus.

Odysseus, who?

Odysseus the last straw, let me in!

Knock Knock!

Who's there?

Goliath.

Goliath, who?

Go-liath down, you look tired.

Knock Knock!

Who's there?

Reign.

Reign, who?

It's reigning kings and queens out here, let me in!

Knock Knock!

Who's there?

History.

History, who?

Knock Knock!

Who's there?

History repeating itself.

Knock Knock!

Who's there?

Toga.

Toga, who?

Toga-ther we can rule the world.

Knock Knock!

Who's there?

Roman.

Roman, who?

Roman around outside is dangerous, come in!

Knock Knock!

Who's there?

Isaac Newton.

Isaac Newton, who?

Isaac knew-tons of things – clever guy!

Knock Knock!

Who's there?

Erik the Red.

Erik the Red, who?

Erik the read about me in the history books?

91

Knock Knock!

Who's there?

Julius Caesar.

Julius Caesar, who?

No, Julius, seize her!
She stole my wallet!

Knock Knock!

Who's there?

Willy.

Willy, who?

Willy compare her
to a summer's day?

Knock Knock!

Who's there?

Toby.

Toby, who?

Wait, sorry, not Toby.

Make up your mind,
who's there?

Toby or not Toby,
that is the question.

Sporty Snorters

Knock Knock!

Who's there?

Adelia.

Adelia, who?

**Adelia cards
and we can
play a game.**

Knock Knock!

Who's there?

Annette.

Annette, who?

**Annette is in
the middle of
a tennis court.**

Knock Knock!

Who's there?

Uriah.

Uriah, who?

Keep Uriah on the ball at all times.

Knock Knock!

Who's there?

A Fred.

A Fred, who?

I'm a Fred I can't play basketball with you today.

Knock Knock!

Who's there?

Tess.

Tess, who?

Tess me the ball, will you?

Knock Knock!

Who's there?

Rene.

Rene, who?

I Rene the marathon this weekend. I'm pooped!

97

Knock knock!

Who's there?

Zeroes.

Zeroes, who?

Zeroes, rows, rows her boat.

Knock Knock!

Who's there?

Les.

Les, who?

Les go for a swim.

Knock Knock!

Who's there?

Falafel.

Falafel, who?

I falafel my skateboard and hurt my knee.

Knock Knock!

Who's there?

Eyesore.

Eyesore, who?

My eye sore from badminton. Ouch!

Knock Knock!

Who's there?

Canoe.

Canoe, who?

Canoe come out and play?

Knock Knock!

Who's there?

Ron.

Ron, who?

Ron a bit faster in your next race.

Knock Knock!

Who's there?

Soccer.

Soccer, who?

**Soccer in
the drawer!**

Knock Knock!

Who's there?

Andy.

Andy, who?

Andy winner is ...

Knock knock!

Who's there?

Ostrich.

Ostrich, who?

Ostrich before a match, don't you?

Knock knock!

Who's there?

Iona.

Iona, who?

Iona new baseball bat, wanna play?

Knock Knock!

Who's there?

Philip.

Philip, who?

Philip the pool, quick!

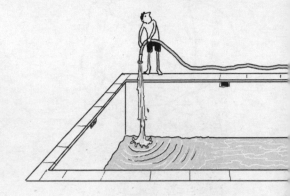

Knock Knock!

Who's there?

Carrot.

Carrot, who?

Carrot-ay chop, hi-yah!

Knock Knock!

Who's there?

Hydrate.

Hydrate, who?

Hydrate your running skills a nine out of ten.

Knock Knock!

Who's there?

Money.

Money, who?

Money hurts from all that jogging.

Knock Knock!

Who's there?

Iced cakes.

Iced cakes, who?

Iced cakes are for hire at the ice rink.

Knock Knock!

Who's there?

Scold.

Scold, who?

Scold enough outside to go ice skating.

Knock Knock!

Who's there?

Lena.

Lena, who?

The Lena Tower
of Pisa.

Knock Knock!

Who's there?

Wa.

Wa, who?

What are you so
excited about?

Knock Knock!

Who's there?

Spell.

Spell, who?

W–H–O.

Knock Knock!

Who's there?

Coffee.

Coffee, who?

No, I'm coughy!
Give me some
medicine!

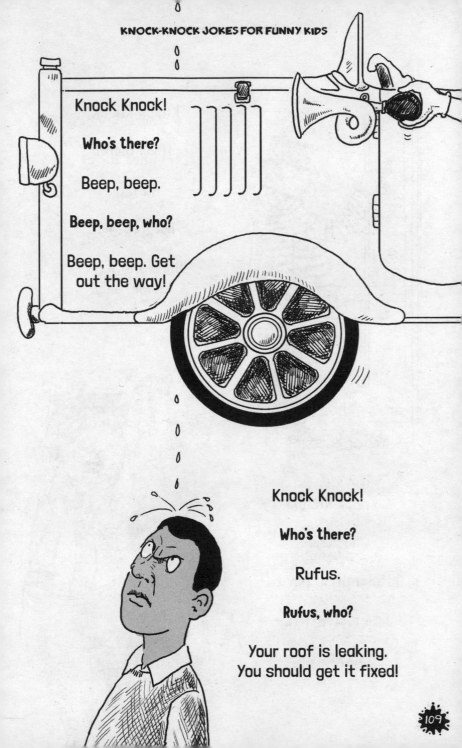

Knock Knock!

Who's there?

Beep, beep.

Beep, beep, who?

Beep, beep. Get out the way!

Knock Knock!

Who's there?

Rufus.

Rufus, who?

Your roof is leaking. You should get it fixed!

Knock Knock!

Who's there?

Burglar.

Burglar, who?

Burglars don't knock, silly.

Knock Knock!

Who's there?

Interrupting pirate.

Interrupting pira—

ARRRRR!

Knock Knock!

Who's there?

I am.

I am, who?

Don't you know
who you are?

Will you remember
me in 5 seconds?

Yes.

Knock Knock!

Who's there?

Hey, you didn't
remember me!

Knock Knock!

Who's there?

Tank.

Tank, who?

You're welcome.

Knock Knock!

Who's there?

Moustache.

Moustache, who?

Moustache you a question, but I'll shave it for later.

Knock Knock!

Who's there?

Uncomfortable silence.

Uncomfortable silence, who?

...

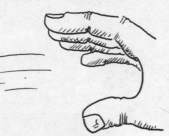

Knock Knock!

Who's there?

A broken pencil.

A broken pencil, who?

Never mind, it's pointless.

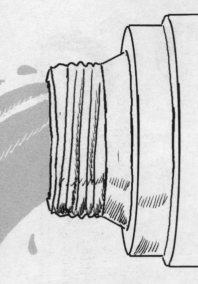

Knock Knock!

Who's there?

Thermos.

Thermos, who?

Thermos be a better joke than this.

Knock Knock!

Who's there?

Icy.

Icy, who?

Icy you!

Knock Knock!

Who's there?

Sorry.

Sorry, who?

Sorry, wrong door.

Knock Knock!

Who's there?

Wooden shoe.

Wooden shoe, who?

Wooden shoe like to hear another joke?

115

Knock Knock!

Who's there?

Stopwatch.

Stopwatch, who?

Stopwatch you're
doing and let me in!

Knock Knock!

Who's there?

Honeydew.

Honeydew, who?

Honeydew
wanna dance?

Knock Knock!

Who's there?

Taco.

Taco, who?

Taco to you later,
you're taking too long
to open the door.

Knock Knock!

Who's there?

Ice cream.

Ice cream, who?

No, you scream!

People
Pleasers

Knock Knock!

Who's there?

Mary.

Mary, who?

Mary Christmas!

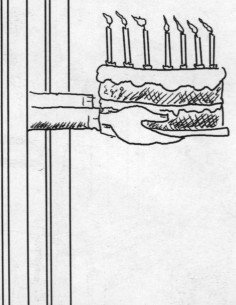

Knock Knock!

Who's there?

Abby.

Abby, who?

Abby birthday to you!

Knock Knock!

Who's there?

Nanna.

Nanna, who?

Nanna your business.

Knock Knock!

Who's there?

Alex.

Alex, who?

Alex-plain later, now let me in!

Knock Knock!

Who's there?

Police.

Police, who?

Police, open up!

Knock Knock!

Who's there?

Police.

Police, who?

Police stop telling these awful knock–knock jokes.

Knock Knock!

Who's there?

Waiter.

Waiter, who?

Waiter I tell you this hilarious joke!

Knock Knock!

Who's there?

Your parents.

Your parents, who?

Your parents who want to know why you locked us out!

Knock Knock!

Who's there?

Ray.

Ray, who?

Ray—member me? I'm your best friend!

Knock Knock!

Who's there?

Doctor.

Doctor Who?

No, just the doctor.

Knock Knock!

Who's there?

Cheese.

Cheese, who?

Cheese my best friend!

Knock Knock!

Who's there?

The electrician.

The electrician, who?

The electrician who's here to fix your doorbell.

Knock Knock!

Who's there?

Butcher.

Butcher, who?

Butcher arms round me and gimme a hug.

Knock Knock!

Who's there?

Sarah.

Sarah, who?

Is Sarah doctor in the house?

Knock Knock!

Who's there?

Farmer.

Farmer, who?

Farmer birthday I'd like a bike, please!

Knock Knock!

Who's there?

Says.

Says, who?

Says me! That's who!

Knock Knock!

Who's there?

Martian.

Martian, who?

Martian around all day is tiring. Can I come in?

Knock Knock!

Who's there?

Rhino.

Rhino, who?

Rhino lots and lots of knock-knock jokes!

ALSO
AVAILABLE:

ISBN: 978-1-78055-784-7 ISBN: 978-1-78055-708-3

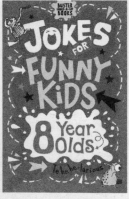

ISBN: 978-1-78055-626-0 ISBN: 978-1-78055-624-6 ISBN: 978-1-78055-625-3